PATRIOTS

AND

LOYALISTS

NATHAN MILOSZEWSKI

PowerKiDS
press
New York

Published in 2020 by The Rosen Publishing Group, Inc.
29 East 21st Street, New York, NY 10010

First Edition

Editor: Jane Katirgis
Book Design: Tanya Dellaccio

Photo Credits: Cover (left) Universal History Archive/Universal Images Group/Getty Images; cover (right) Ipsumpix/Corbis Historical/Getty Images; p. 5 (inset) https://upload.wikimedia.org/wikipedia/commons/b/b9/Sons_of_Liberty_Broadside%2C_1765.jpg; p. 5 (main) GraphicaArtis/Archive Photos/Getty Images; p. 7 dikobraziy/Shutterstock.com; p. 9 (top) Joe Sohm/Visions of America/Universal Images Group/Getty Images; pp. 9 (bottom), 15 (tarring and feathering image) Bettmann/Getty Images; pp. 11, 13 Stock Montage/Archive Photos/Getty Images; p. 15 (Thomas Hutchinson) https://upload.wikimedia.org/wikipedia/commons/0/0f/ThomasHutchinsonByEdwardTruman.jpg; p. 17 (arrest of William Franklin) Print Collector/Hulton Archive/Getty Images; p. 17 (Ben Franklin) https://upload.wikimedia.org/wikipedia/commons/2/25/Benjamin_Franklin_by_Joseph_Duplessis_1778.jpg; p. 19 Barney Burstein/Corbis Historical/Getty Images; pp. 21, 27 (main) Historical/Corbis Historical/Getty Images; p. 23 (Thomas Paine) Hulton Archive/Getty Images; p. 23 (Common Sense cover) https://upload.wikimedia.org/wikipedia/commons/4/4a/Commonsense.jpg; p. 25 Time Life Pictures/The LIFE Picture Collection/Getty Images; p. 27 (inset) Courtesy of The New York Public Library; p. 29 https://upload.wikimedia.org/wikipedia/commons/9/94/Harper%27s_New_Monthly_Magazine_Volume_104_December_1901_to_May_1902_%281902%29_%2814596618078%29.jpg; p. 30 https://upload.wikimedia.org/wikipedia/commons/a/a6/Treaty_of_Paris_1783_-_last_page_%28hi-res%29.jpg.

Cataloging-in-Publication Data

Names: Miloszewski, Nathan.
Title: Patriots and Loyalists / Nathan Miloszewski.
Description: New York : PowerKids Press, 2019. | Series: Opponents in American history | Includes glossary and index.
Identifiers: ISBN 9781538345443 (pbk.) | ISBN 9781538343692 (library bound) | ISBN 9781538345450 (6pack)
Subjects: LCSH: Revolutionaries—United States—History—18th century—Juvenile literature. | American loyalists—United States—History—18th century—Juvenile literature. | United States—History—Revolution, 1775–1783—Juvenile literature. | United States–History—Revolution, 1775-1783—Social aspects—Juvenile literature.
Classification: LCC E208.M55 2020 | DDC 973.3—dc23

Manufactured in the United States of America

CPSIA Compliance Information: Batch # #CSPK19. For Further Information contact Rosen Publishing, New York, New York at 1-800-237-9932

CONTENTS

REVOLUTIONARY SPLIT

Before the 13 British colonies in North America became the United States, they were ruled by Great Britain. Eventually, people in North America started to feel they were being taken advantage of by the British government. Some wanted independence and were willing to fight for it. They became known as patriots. The patriots wanted liberty and the freedom to govern themselves.

Not everyone agreed with the American patriots. Some people felt that life was good under British rule, and they remained loyal to King George III. Members of this group became known as Loyalists.

Anger against the British grew so strong that it became unsafe for Loyalists to declare their **allegiance** in public. In 1776, the 13 colonies declared independence from Great Britain. The American Revolutionary War was about to begin.

TAXATION WITHOUT REPRESENTATION

"Taxation without representation" summed up part of how the American colonists felt about how they were treated by the British government. The colonies had no representation in the British Parliament, or lawmaking body, which passed laws they considered unfair. This was a major cause of the American Revolutionary War.

THE SONS OF LIBERTY WAS A GROUP OF AMERICAN PATRIOTS. THEY WERE RESPONSIBLE FOR **REBELLIOUS** ACTS SUCH AS THE BOSTON TEA PARTY. THIS ANNOUNCEMENT CALLED FOR THEM TO MEET TO "HEAR THE PUBLIC RESIGNATION" OF AN UNPOPULAR TAX COLLECTOR.

St—p! St—p! St—p! No:

Tuesday-Morning, December 17, 1765.

THE True-born Sons of Liberty, are desired to meet under LIBERTY-TREE, at XII o'Clock, THIS DAY, to hear the public Resignation, under Oath, of ANDREW OLIVER, Esq; Distributor of Stamps for the Province of the *Massachusetts-Bay.*

A Resignation ? YES.

NEGLECT AND THE
SEEDS OF INDEPENDENCE

For the American colonies, much of the 1700s was a period of self-rule with little interference from Great Britain. The colonies enjoyed freedom as long as they were loyal to the king, continued to be good trade partners, and made a lot of money for Britain.

This unwritten policy was known as "salutary neglect." This means the British government was **intentionally** not paying much attention to the colonies and not enforcing trade laws and regulations.

People in the colonies became used to taking care of themselves without being told what to do by Great Britain. That started to change when Britain wanted more control and needed more money. The government began enforcing laws and demanding new taxes. This angered the colonists, who felt the government didn't have the authority to do that.

AMERICAN COLONISTS RELIED ON INTERNATIONAL TRADE TO MAKE MONEY AND BUY GOODS THEY NEEDED. AMERICA SOLD RAW MATERIALS AND BOUGHT MANUFACTURED GOODS FROM BRITAIN. BUT THE SYSTEM WAS SET UP SO THAT AMERICANS BOUGHT MORE FROM THE BRITISH THAN THEY SOLD TO THEM, WHICH CREATED AN UNFAIR TRADING RELATIONSHIP.

Great Britain passed the Navigation Acts of the 1600s to prevent the colonies from trading with other countries. These laws were meant to control trade and make more money for Britain. However, they greatly angered Americans.

← **COLONIAL IMPORTS**

← **COLONIAL EXPORTS**

← **INTERCOLONIAL TRADE**

NORTH AMERICA

GREAT BRITAIN

13 BRITISH COLONIES

EUROPE

ATLANTIC OCEAN

WEST INDIES

AFRICA

SOUTH AMERICA

WHO WERE THE PATRIOTS?

Famous patriots included well-known Founding Fathers such as George Washington, Thomas Jefferson, Alexander Hamilton, John Adams, Samuel Adams, and Benjamin Franklin. These men were part of the group that was responsible for creating the Declaration of Independence and the U.S. Constitution.

The patriots also included regular working-class people such as laborers and farmers. Some of these people were inspired to join the Continental army led by General George Washington or to help the cause in other ways.

Washington used a network, or chain, of ordinary citizens across the country to work **undercover** as spies. These patriots gathered useful information they overheard from the British as they went about their everyday lives, working in shops and taverns or delivering goods. Patriot spies also spread false information about how big Washington's army was to trick the British into thinking they were fighting a much stronger foe.

NATHAN HALE WAS A CAPTAIN IN THE CONTINENTAL ARMY. HE VOLUNTEERED FOR A SPY MISSION TO TRACK THE MOVEMENTS OF BRITISH TROOPS. IN ONE MISSION, HE PRETENDED TO BE A TEACHER WHILE HE GATHERED INFORMATION. HE WAS CAUGHT WITH MAPS AND DRAWINGS OF TROOP LOCATIONS. THE BRITISH EXECUTED HIM AS A SPY ON SEPTEMBER 22, 1776. HALE IS THE OFFICIAL STATE HERO OF CONNECTICUT.

HEAD TO HEAD

Patriots were also called revolutionaries, Continentals, rebels, or American Whigs. The patriot army was called the Continental army, and the Whigs were a political group that opposed the Tory group in Great Britain.

9

WHO WERE THE LOYALISTS?

The Loyalists, American colonists who supported the British monarchy and British rule of the colonies, were also called Tories or Royalists. Loyalists were often wealthy merchants and businessmen who lived in port cities such as New York City and Boston. While many Loyalists often had ties to the **elite** class back in Great Britain, their supporters also included some farmers, immigrants, slaves, and Native Americans. There were people of all class levels on both sides of the conflict.

Loyalists had several reasons for not wanting to break away from Britain. Some simply wanted to remain British citizens and felt the patriots wouldn't be able to run the country as well as Great Britain did. Some didn't want to ruin their existing business interests, which included a very profitable global trade network.

HEAD TO HEAD

Patriots nicknamed the Loyalists "Tories" as an insult because the label has ties to an Irish word for "outlaw."

MANY LOYALISTS AREN'T REMEMBERED BECAUSE THEY DIDN'T WIN THE WAR. BENEDICT ARNOLD IS WELL KNOWN BECAUSE HE SWITCHED SIDES. ARNOLD IS SHOWN HERE AS HE SLIPS SECRET INFORMATION TO JOHN ANDRE, A BRITISH OFFICER LATER HANGED AS A SPY BY THE CONTINENTAL ARMY.

THE MOST FAMOUS TRAITOR

Benedict Arnold started off as a member of the Continental army. Although he fought heroically, he was passed over for a promotion to a higher rank. Arnold thought the patriots weren't grateful for his talents. He began giving secret information, such as U.S. troop locations, to the British. His actions so angered the patriots that it gave them new energy to keep fighting. To this day, his name is used to mean "traitor" in the United States.

11

FENCE SITTERS

If you weren't a patriot or a Loyalist during this era, you might be seen as a "fence sitter" who didn't want to pick a side. People who stayed out of the conflict may have done so because it was safer not to openly declare an allegiance to one side or the other.

It has been said that when the Revolutionary War started, one-third of the colonists were for it, one-third were against it, and the last third of the colonists were **neutral**. However, in reality, the majority of colonists were fence sitters. Both patriots and Loyalists tried to win their support because getting popular opinion on their side could help change the outcome. In the end, many American colonists ended up choosing the side that benefited them the most, either for personal or business reasons.

BRITAIN EXPECTED MORE

When the war started, leaders in Great Britain had the false sense they would receive lots of help from Loyalists in the colonies. They thought Loyalists could be relied on to join their army in great numbers, especially in the South. Loyalists did serve as soldiers, but there weren't as many as Great Britain had hoped for. This didn't help British **strategy** during the war.

MOST COLONISTS WERE NEUTRAL FENCE SITTERS AT THE BEGINNING OF THE AMERICAN REVOLUTIONARY WAR. BOTH LOYALISTS AND PATRIOTS TRIED TO WIN THEIR SUPPORT. THIS ILLUSTRATION DEPICTS GENERAL GEORGE WASHINGTON LEADING THE CONTINENTAL ARMY IN THE BATTLE OF PRINCETON DURING THE WAR.

13

PUBLIC HUMILIATION

Patriots often weren't kind to Loyalists. If a patriot found out someone supported Great Britain, they might insult the person in public or do worse. Gangs attacked Loyalists, people seized their land, and patriots **vandalized** their property or set it on fire.

Patriot threats sometimes forced Loyalists to flee their homes. Unless British troops were nearby to protect them, Loyalists faced cruel punishments such as tarring and feathering.

This treatment wasn't just because they were on different sides. Patriots were warning Loyalists who were acting as spies, sending information and supplies to help the British troops. Because independence was at stake, patriots felt they needed to create a sense of fear to keep the British from gaining any type of advantage.

HEAD TO HEAD

Before Benedict Arnold switched sides, the most hated Loyalist in America was Thomas Hutchinson, governor of Massachusetts. His likeness was burned many times because of his Loyalist views.

PATRIOTS ARE SHOWN AFTER TARRING AND FEATHERING A LOYALIST. THEY'RE PREPARING TO POUR TEA INTO HIS MOUTH. THE CUT ROPE AND STRUCTURE BEHIND THE MEN SHOW THAT THE PATRIOTS FIRST THREATENED THE LOYALIST WITH HANGING.

THOMAS HUTCHINSON

FOUNDING FATHER VS. SON

Despite their differences, both sides had much in common. Sometimes Loyalists and patriots were from the same families. Benjamin Franklin's son, William Franklin, was a Loyalist and the royal governor of New Jersey.

Benjamin tried to convince his son to join the patriot cause, but William was loyal to the king. The younger Franklin thought Americans wouldn't support the Revolution. He was placed in a Connecticut jail for two years for the actions he took to help the British. After he was exchanged for a patriot prisoner, he moved first to New York City and then to Great Britain. He never returned to the American colonies and continued to promote the idea that Britain should keep fighting to take back control of the colonies.

FAMILIES DIVIDED

*Stephen Jarvis, a young Connecticut farmhand, joined a patriot **militia** whose commander was his uncle. Stephen said he did this to anger his father (and maybe to impress his girlfriend). However, he changed his mind and joined the Queen's American Rangers, a Loyalist military unit. After the war, he expected to return home. But after a mob attacked his father's house, Stephen and his family moved to Canada.*

The political divide between the Franklins damaged their relationship for the rest of their lives. Although they were close before the war, they didn't speak much afterward. Benjamin only saw his son one more time while on a trip through Great Britain.

BENJAMIN FRANKLIN

BENJAMIN FRANKLIN TRIED TO CONVINCE HIS SON TO JOIN THE PATRIOTS. WILLIAM REFUSED AND WAS JAILED FOR BEING A LOYALIST. HIS FATHER, WHO FELT HURT BY HIS SON'S ACTIONS, DID NOTHING TO HELP HIM. THEIR ONCE-CLOSE RELATIONSHIP WAS RUINED AND NEVER REPAIRED.

17

THE BOSTON MASSACRE

It was the night of March 5, 1770. When British soldiers opened fire on an angry mob protesting taxes on imported goods, it became one of the key events that helped turn American colonists against their British rulers.

Five colonists died and a handful of others were injured. Patriots called this event "the Boston **Massacre**," but the British simply called it "the incident on King Street." Afterward, both sides used this as **propaganda** in the media to prove that the other side was at fault.

The patriots weren't as innocent in this case as they're sometimes made out to be. They were guilty of **rioting** and trying to start a fight with the soldiers. The crowd taunted the soldiers and threw snowballs, ice, sticks, and oyster shells at them.

A PATRIOT DEFENDS THE BRITISH SOLDIERS

Eight British soldiers involved in the Boston Massacre were tried for murder before a jury. Patriot and Founding Father John Adams took on the case as their defense lawyer. No matter their differences, he wanted to make sure they had a fair trial. Adams successfully convinced juries that five of the soldiers were not guilty, on the grounds that their lives were in danger and they had the right to defend themselves.

THIS ENGRAVING BY PAUL REVERE, *THE BLOODY MASSACRE IN KING-STREET*, WAS QUICKLY PASSED AROUND THE COLONIES. IT HELPED TO FUEL AMERICAN ANGER AGAINST THE BRITISH.

THE BOSTON TEA PARTY

In 1773, Great Britain passed the Tea Act, which allowed the British East India Company the sole right to import and sell tea in the colonies. This cut out colonial merchants and tea smugglers and kept an earlier tax on tea, although it made British tea cheaper as a whole. Colonists were still angry about taxation without representation. On December 16, 1773, a band of patriots boarded ships in Boston Harbor and dumped a great deal of tea into the water.

John Adams called this organized act "the most magnificent Movement of all" because it was such a bold move by the patriots. Loyalists lost a lot of money because of the Tea Party. The event helped to inspire more Americans to fight for their independence.

THIS ENGRAVING FROM 1789 SHOWS AMERICAN COLONISTS DUMPING CHESTS OF TEA OWNED BY THE BRITISH EAST INDIA COMPANY INTO BOSTON HARBOR.

HEAD TO HEAD

After the patriots dumped 342 chests of tea (over 90,000 pounds) into the water, Boston Harbor smelled like tea for weeks.

COMMON SENSE
REJECTS THE CROWN

In 1776, Thomas Paine published *Common Sense*, a **pamphlet** that helped create support for the American Revolution. It was originally printed **anonymously** so that Paine could avoid being accused of treason. Speaking out against the king of Great Britain could mean torture or death.

Many people read the pamphlet. It had a powerful influence on patriots, encouraging them to fight for a government that would give them equal rights and opportunities.

Loyalists were caught off guard by the response to *Common Sense*. They thought many colonists were being misled by a piece of propaganda. In response, James Chalmers, a Maryland Loyalist, wrote *Plain Truth* to reject the ideas of *Common Sense* and explain why Great Britain was still the colonies' ruler. However, Chalmers's writing style wasn't as easy to understand.

Thomas Paine donated any money made from sales of *Common Sense* to help fund the Continental army.

COMMON SENSE;

ADDRESSED TO THE *W. Hamilton*

INHABITANTS

OF

AMERICA,

On the following interesting

SUBJECTS.

I. Of the Origin and Design of Government in general, with concise Remarks on the English Constitution.

II. Of Monarchy and Hereditary Succession.

III. Thoughts on the present State of American Affairs.

IV. Of the present Ability of America, with some miscellaneous Reflections.

Thomas Paine

Man knows no Master save creating HEAVEN, Or those whom choice and common good ordain.

THOMSON.

COMMON SENSE WAS VERY SUCCESSFUL. IT SOLD WELL, WAS EASY TO READ AND UNDERSTAND, AND CONVINCED MANY AMERICANS TO FIGHT FOR INDEPENDENCE.

DRIFTING AWAY FROM BRITAIN

One of the major events that led Americans to start believing that Great Britain didn't have the right to rule them anymore was the aftermath of the French and Indian War, fought in North America between Britain and France from 1754 to 1763. The war was very expensive, so Britain wanted to increase taxes on Americans to help pay for it. Colonists were expected to pay for housing British troops after the war, and colonists were prevented from moving farther west into the continent.

23

THE AMERICAN REVOLUTION

At the beginning of the revolution, patriots were excited to join the Continental army. But as the war continued, signing bonuses and the promise of free land were needed to attract more men. Conditions were tough, and there wasn't enough money or supplies.

Some Continental army soldiers became jealous of ordinary citizens, thinking they had it easy and weren't sacrificing enough for the cause. Some soldiers rebelled near the end of the war due to a lack of pay.

American Loyalists who joined the British forces didn't have it much easier. A captured Tory soldier was considered a traitor, so he might be sent to live on the frontier, imprisoned with no chance of getting out, or killed. Even their British officers looked down on them.

LOYALISTS LEFT BEHIND

British General Charles Cornwallis surrendered at Yorktown in 1781. As part of the truce, George Washington demanded that Tories fighting with the British be handed over as prisoners of state. This meant they would be treated as criminals. As Cornwallis sailed away after the war, hundreds of desperate Loyalists rowed after his ship, fearing for their lives. Most were turned away and captured by the patriots.

24

THIS ENGRAVING SHOWS THE 1775 BATTLE OF BUNKER HILL, ONE OF THE EARLY BATTLES OF THE REVOLUTIONARY WAR.

HEAD TO HEAD

After patriots tore down the statue of King George III in New York City on July 9, 1776, they melted parts of it and made bullets to use against the British.

COMPETING FOR ALLIES

Patriots and Loyalists both competed for the allegiances of slaves and Native Americans. Slaves were promised freedom for their efforts in the war. Native American tribes chose sides based on their trading relationships and a desire to protect their lands and liberties.

More Native Americans helped the British than the patriots based on promises that Great Britain would prevent colonists from moving into their territory. Before the war, American colonists ignored British orders and took native land. Many tribes tried to stay neutral. However, as the war spread, they felt compelled to join the fight.

Some slaves fought in place of their patriot masters with the understanding this would earn them their freedom. Other slaves ran away to join the British forces, some of which promised freedom.

HEAD TO HEAD

After the war, only a few slaves on either side were rewarded with freedom. Both sides went back on promises and many slaves were returned to their masters.

MARQUIS DE LAFAYETTE, A FRENCH GENERAL WHO FOUGHT IN THE REVOLUTIONARY WAR WITH THE PATRIOTS, RECRUITED A SLAVE, JAMES ARMISTEAD, TO BE A SPY TO PROVIDE HIM INFORMATION ABOUT THE BRITISH TROOPS. IN THIS LETTER, LAFAYETTE TESTIFIES ABOUT HOW BRAVELY ARMISTEAD SERVED. HE WAS FREED AND LATER RENAMED HIMSELF WITH LAFAYETTE'S LAST NAME TO HONOR THE GENERAL.

After the war, many Loyalists decided to leave the new United States. Some wealthy Loyalists went back to Great Britain, where they still had family and business interests. Others moved to Canada, where they were given land in return for their loyalty. About 80,000 to 100,000 Loyalists left the former 13 colonies after the Revolutionary War.

Even if they wanted to stay in the United States, Loyalists often felt very unwelcome. Many patriots considered them to be traitors. Some Loyalists did want to stay because they had built their lives there. With their wealth and education, Loyalists could have been a help to society, but many felt they had to leave. Loyalists who did stay had to be quiet to stay safe.

THIS 1901 ILLUSTRATION BY HOWARD PYLE, *TORY REFUGEES ON THEIR WAY TO CANADA*, SHOWS THE DISLIKE AND ANGER PATRIOTS HAD TOWARD LOYALISTS. IN THE BACKGROUND, PATRIOTS HURL ROCKS AT THE DEPARTING LOYALISTS.

29

PEACE BETWEEN
NATIONS BUT NOT PEOPLE

The Treaty of Paris of 1783 ended the war between Great Britain and America, but there was no peace between patriots and Loyalists. The patriots were the winners, but they didn't forgive and forget. They often wouldn't let their disagreements with the Loyalists end. Loyalists who stayed in America were attacked so much that Great Britain asked that the Treaty of Paris include protection for them.

We don't know much about Loyalists because their side of the story wasn't written about as much. However, the patriot revolt wasn't always as popular as it's made out to be. Even John Adams, a Founding Father, once thought that the ideas from Thomas Paine's *Common Sense* were too radical, or very bold and extreme.

TREATY OF
PARIS

GLOSSARY

allegiance: Loyalty to a person, group, or cause.

anonymously: Not named or identified.

elite: The people in a society who are thought to be the greatest.

intentionally: With intention, or a certain aim or plan.

massacre: The violent killing of many people.

militia: A group of people who are not an official part of the armed forces of a country but are trained like soldiers.

neutral: Not taking sides.

pamphlet: A short printed publication with no cover or with a paper cover.

propaganda: Ideas or statements, often false or exaggerated, that are spread to help a cause.

rebellious: Inclined to fight against authority.

riot: A violent public disturbance by a group of people.

strategy: A plan of action to achieve a goal.

undercover: Collecting information in secret.

vandalize: To damage or destroy something on purpose.

INDEX

WEBSITES

Due to the changing nature of Internet links, PowerKids Press has developed an online list of websites related to the subject of this book. This site is updated regularly. Please use this link to access the list: www.powerkidslinks.com/oiah/patriot